PHARAOH

RESURRECTED

JOHN M. GARDNER

ॐ

CONTAINING

A Romantic but Real Story about the Discovery of the First Royal Tomb with a Pharaoh and its Contents Intact

AND

Historical Review Leading to the Discovery of the Tomb of
TUT - ANKH - AMEN

WITH ILLUSTRATIONS INCLUDING THOSE TAKEN BY AUTHOR IN THE TOMBS, WITH SPECIAL PERMISSION OF EGYPTIAN GOVERNMENT

NEW YORK
SORG PUBLISHING CO.
1923

Kessinger Publishing's Rare Reprints
Thousands of Scarce and Hard-to-Find Books!

Type of interior of a Royal Mausoleum

CONTENTS

CHAPTER I

Revival of the World's Interest in the Tombs of Ancient Egypt

THE recent discovery of the tomb of TUT-ANKH-AMEN at Thebes, near Luxor, Egypt, has riveted the attention of the world and focused it upon this great dramatic scene. Those who have not visited Luxor, or closely studied the situation as it presents itself there today, as well as the preceding events, commencing in July, 1881, all of which are but one chapter of historical discovery, naturally seek light upon the subject. The ordinary imagination is hardly strong enough to picture the enormous wealth and importance of these discoveries. We are prone to believe that the sight of a human body in quite perfect form, dead more than three thousand years, surrounded by their personal effects in perfect condition, is an impossibility; but, that is the very condition which the Egyptian Tombs of the Pharaohs and their contents are exhibiting today, and have been doing since 1881.

It must be borne in mind that Greece, Rome and Europe are comparatively modern places and were not in active existence when Egypt was in the zenith of its power. It is, therefore, an amazing experience, when we, living thirty-five or more centuries after the Theban tombs were dug, can unlock them and find intact the priceless treasures, consisting of the bodies of its greatest Monarchs, perfectly preserved, even with their hair, teeth, and finger-nails, and wrapped in their robes of state, containing their detail history in scrolls of papyri. More than that, to find their favorite chariots, household belongings, chairs, tables, dishes, vases, beds, couches, and even *thrones,* all beautifully gilded, carved and inlaid, as became the dignity of their royal ownership, is inexpressibly marvelous. To think that here are Pharaohs who reigned with the highest glory and power, and more than fourteen hundred years before Christ, accompanied with all their personal belongings, as though but buried yesterday, and in perfect form, puts us in mental, spiritual, as well as physical contact, with their actual life. It is because of this great fact, attested by as indisputable evidence of authenticity, as that the world itself existed in their day, that makes these sepulchres and their treasures, of transcendent interest and importance, surpassing in depth of human interest, any discovery ever made, except perhaps, that of America by Columbus. Of course, it is well known, that the great pyramids were long since outstanding monuments to the

[6]

engineering skill and perfection of mechanical appliances, astronomical knowledge, and highest order of civilization prevailing among the Egyptians over forty centuries ago. In fact, they have never been equalled in massiveness of construction or majesty of appearance by anything ever erected on earth, of which we have any account. To look upon the great pyramid of Cheops from Cairo, only a few miles distant, which, with others of nearly equal proportions, looms up against a yellowish twilight sky at the dawn of evening, presents a picture of silent and picturesque grandeur unequalled by anything in the world. It is interesting to note that Cheops, who preceded Rameses the Great, thousands of years, built it for his tomb. In the heart of it is a great sarcophagus in which his body was laid, but disappeared many centuries even before Thebes was founded, five hundred miles up the Nile. It seems to have been a dominant passion with the Egyptian Monarchs to perpetuate their memories by their tombs and temples and the inscriptions engraven thereon. In this they have succeeded. That which happened in the discovery of the so-called Rassul Tomb in 1881, and is happening up to this very day, in finding royal sepulchres of the Pharaohs with their body and belongings intact, is naturally what they, in the dim past would, and undoubtedly did, expect to happen. No doubt the world to which they thought their bodies and souls would some day return, *is the world* in which *we* now *live*. We certainly have got their

Passion of the Pharaohs to perpetuate their memories by monuments and tombs.

*The God of
Fashion
reproducing
Pharaoh's
belongings.*

thrones, chariots, jewelry, household belongings
and their most cherished, personal possessions,
and their bodies. It would not be surprising
that the God of Fashion to which the inhabitants of the present world bow with such abject
obeisance and admiration, will ornament Society
and its devotees with reproductions of the sacred
belongings of the Pharaohs, and thus revive
again the material life of those proud Monarchs.
We hope, however, if the material part of their
existence is handed out to us by the God of
Fashion for our obeisance, that we will not
suffer the return, at least of the souls of Rameses
the Great or his successor, Menephtah. They
were the Pharaohs of the Exodus and of the
Bondage. The Bible as all readers know, fully
describes the awful and inhuman deeds of
Menephtah, who ruled over Egypt oppressing
the Jews and killing their first born, with a
severity almost unbelievable, finally driving them
out of the land through the Red Sea. (See
Exodus, Chapters 12 to 16.)

*Bible references
to the Pharaohs
found.*

    As to Rameses the Great, he has always been
known as the Pharaoh of the Bondage, one
whose acts of cruelty and oppression are unparalleled in human history, one who treated
human beings as beasts of burden, grinding them
down and extinguishing them with such blood
thirsty passion as to make even Nero blush with
shame. Of him and his deeds Moses again
wrote so many times that the civilized world
has become as familiar with him in Biblical

[8]

history as with any of the great Prophets. (See Exodus, Chapters 7 to 12.)

Pharaohs of the Bondage and Exodus now with us.

The bodies of these great Monarchs have been found, the latter in the Rassul tomb, and today he lies in his robes of State, in his Imperial coffin with all his features and body quite as perfect as the day when he died. Think of it! Here are his hands, fingers, finger-nails, ears, nose, lips, teeth, hair upon his head, body, with its normal flesh, only hardened, with almost its normal color, eye-brows, closed eyes. He looks as though he is but sleeping, under a heavy plate glass, as you look upon him in the lambent light of a silent room in the Cairo Museum. Then again, near him in the midst of such Imperial splendor and impressive silence, lies Menephtah, exposed to the gaze and awe striking wonder of the World. It takes but a moment of reflection to awaken deeply a proper appreciation of what this great scene means to us of the Twentieth Century. Thus, suppose some day it should be reported that *Job* or *Joshua* or *Abraham* or *Moses,* or *Solomon,* either one, or all, were found in some Assyrian tomb with their bodies in perfect form, lying in the coffins in which they were buried. Then again, assume there should be wrapped about their bodies parchment or linen on which should be written in the language of their day the main facts of their lives, perfectly preserved, and coinciding with the facts of their Biblical history—how overwhelmingly sensational and awe-striking would be such an experience to the normal mind of man. *In fact,* it

More sensational than if Moses or Solomon found.

[9]

would seem more like a wild dream than a real fact. The instinct of skepticism would at once assert itself and involuntarily *repel the idea of actuality.* And yet such is the condition with which we are confronted today in the resurrection of the Royal tombs with the bodies, and Imperial trappings of the Pharaohs of the Exodus and Bondage. Even more so, would it seem unbelievable in the case of the Pharaohs because some of them flourished and died Centuries before Moses and the Prophets, and then again, because they played greater parts in the ancient drama of the World's activities and experiences, than these Biblical characters. There remains of course, but one great thing which must be established, in order to take us out of our dreamy, and half skeptical impressions and make us consciously realize the actuality of this great fact, and that is, the *indisputable authenticity* of the history which unfolds it to us. When that is accomplished, interest deepens and our attention is *riveted* and so fastened to the historical object or experience that we are only then fully aroused to a just sense of appreciation. It will, therefore, be our effort to take our readers out of dreamland and place before them such *indisputable* facts as show that the world is not *fooled;* that, the material parts of the great Pharaohs have returned to us and that, we too, of the Twentieth Century are living in their midst as did their contemporaries *more than thirty centuries ago.* We see the same golden chariot, that rolled over the pavements of ancient

[10]

Thebes with Pharaoh in it, the sound and sight of which caused a roar of plaudits from the populace. We see the harness and trappings of the stamping steeds which bore it on, the canopies which shielded him from the same heated sun which yet burns from the Egyptian sky. We see the couches upon which he rested when floating up and down the Nile amidst the acclaim of the millions on its shores, and above all the same triumphant Pharaohs with their bodies but little changed.

The real hero of our story is Abd-er-Rassul, a simple Arab, living in a cave on the fringe of the Theban Plains, the first discoverer of a Royal tomb with its Pharaoh and contents made in over thirty centuries, in the Summer of 1875. The life of this simple Arab, the manner in which he discovered the tomb containing the most historic and valuable contents of any of which there is an account in ancient or modern history, and the clew he gave, which has led to the discovery of the several tombs since 1875, including that of the recent one of Tut-ankh-Amen, we will refer to later on. At present, however, it is our desire to acquaint the reader with the general features of Egypt and the field in which the great drama is being enacted today, in order to view the subject from its proper surroundings and the atmosphere in which it is exhibited.

Arab cavedweller, discoverer of first Royal tomb.

CHAPTER II

General Survey of Egypt, the Cradle of Civilization

EGYPT has been accredited as being the "Cradle" of the civilization of the world. One in America, or elsewhere, not having visited the land of the Pharaohs, is quite apt to get an impression that it consists mostly of waste and desert land, with a few old mouldering temples and tombs, with now and then an occasional tablet or inscription which faintly voices the history of the past, but this is all a mistake. No more fertile valley in the world exists than that of the Nile, stretching from its delta terminus, near Alexandria, and extending southward as far as Assuan, the place of the first cataract. The Nile is not, as sometimes supposed, a mud creek, but is a great navigable stream, upon which for most of the distance large steamers can ply. It varies in width from one-half to three miles. Unlike any other river, it has no tributaries flowing into it from mountain sides or adjoining valleys. This great valley extends on either side of the river, at least as

Nile valley most fertile in the world.

INTERIOR OF A ROYAL TOMB

far as Luxor, several hundred miles south. It varies in width, extending on either side of the river from three to seven miles. Skirting the valley are two great ranges of mountains, which are treeless, being but great lime stone rocks and running almost parallel with each other, north and south, presenting to the eye, when seen from a steamer, a very picturesque sight. Thus is seen, on either side, the green, luxurious valley, and off in the distance, piercing the blue, cloudless skies, these great ranges of mountains, which seem to run as regularly and continuously as the river itself. There is much that interested us about the great pyramids of Gizeh, near Cairo, one-half hour's ride therefrom, and looming up in the distance a few miles from the city, with a picturesqueness and grandeur seldom witnessed anywhere. We thought, when contemplating these vast structures, erected by human hands several thousands of years B. C., upon geometrical lines as perfect as human genius could make them today, we had found Egypt's greatest point of interest and its most interesting monuments of antiquity. In fact, we believe that the traveler generally is thus impressed, when one has not penetrated farther into the interior of this classic country. Many are therefore influenced to go no further and to be content with looking upon the monument of Cheops, erected to immortalize himself, and to view the Sphinx, partly buried beneath the hot sands, with its broken nose and ears. They, too, are content with visiting at Sakkara, the

Nile Valley a green and very rich agricultural land.

The pyramids link 19th century to remote antiquity.

[13]

tombs of the sacred Bulls, and old Memphis nearby, with a prostrate statue of Rameses the Great, of colossal size, lying under the shade of a palm grove. It is true that these of themselves are witnesses sufficient to convince the mind, of the glory and Imperial majesty of the First Dynasty.

Of course, although Cairo is eight or nine hundred years old, it is considered a modern city in Egypt. In fact, it has no interest, as a city of antiquities, but is fast becoming the great social center for Europeans in Winter. The Museum at Cairo is the first in all the world for great and priceless antiquities. In this wonderful structure are to be found relics commencing with the pre-historic period more than three thousand years B. C. It is inexhaustible in its interesting exhibition of things of the past. One finds himself walking through great corridors, surrounded on every hand by engraven tablets, painted masks, in beautiful colors, coffins and articles of domestic furniture, excavated from the tombs of all ages, and feels that he is living in the past, several thousand years ago. In fact, the Museum is so varied, inexhaustible and extensive, that one, in looking upon the ancient arts, sciences and material life, exhibited here, may well imagine himself to be an Egyptian six thousand years old, standing upon the pinnacle of the present age and going back, with one grand vision, over the vast vista of past ages and beholding most of that which was the pride and

In Cairo Museum, one looks back 6,000 years at Egyptian arts and Sciences.

glory of his country in matters of art and science.

Proceeding now from Cairo and vicinity to Luxor, and Thebes, where the Rassul tomb was found in 1875, and out of which its contents were taken in 1881, and where the tomb of Tut-ankh-Amen is now being excavated, passing by some interesting centers on the way, with which we do not wish to unduly burden our account, we at last arrived there, which must be borne in mind, is several hundred miles up the Nile. Luxor is the site of ancient Thebes, a city said to contain more than 4,000,000 inhabitants, with a hundred golden gates, often the subject of poetic song by the classic poets of antiquity. This great city was divided by the Nile, as the Borough of Manhattan by the East River, is from Brooklyn. The site of Luxor is on the east bank. On this side of the river is to be found many of the greatest temples that ever existed in the world, notably those of Luxor and Karnak, and *no tombs,* while on the west side are the famous Royal tombs, mostly in a mountain, besides many great temples. This is due to the fact that the "Westminster" of Egypt or the "Greenwood" of Thebes, was in the "Borough" (to use the modern language of today), on the west side of the river. Here it was that the Pharaoh of the Bondage Rameses the Great, as well as of the Exodus, Menephtah, and Seti the First, the father of Rameses, and others of nearly equal fame, luxuriated in their palaces. Traces of these are yet seen. They

Ancient Thebes had 4,000,000 people.

Famous Royal Tombs are in a rocky mountain.

wielded those scepters of power that awed the whole world and whose worldly pomp and pagan grandeur were a hundred times flayed by the scriptural pen of the Prophets.

The first to charm us at Luxor, to divert ourselves somewhat from the tombs, are its temples. Let us before crossing the river, make note of the two great ones, those of Karnak and Luxor. The former covers an area of more than twenty acres and that of Luxor more than ten. So well have they been preserved by the heaps of dirt and sand under which they have been buried for thirty centuries or more, that the engraven inscriptions and symbols upon their massive columns and solid masonry appear as sharp and readable as though imprinted but yesterday. The question is how it came to happen, that these temples slept so silently and for so long and have only come to light so recently, and mostly within the last fifty years. Especially does this seem marvelous in view of an unbroken continuity of human government and civilization existing here since their original construction. More strange yet does it seem when we learn, even from Herodotus, that so far back as four and five hundred years B. C., that this spot was visited by European travelers, who journeyed here to view the wondrous relics then standing of antiquity, these very obelisks, the colossi of Thebes and the various temples. This is verified by occasional inscriptions in Greek and Latin, made several hundred years B. C., found upon the great stones. The explanation is

One temple alone covers more than 20 acres.

this: After the decline of the New Empire (1324 B. C.), the invasion of foreigners became constant and increasingly powerful, while the worship in the temples gradually lessened, until finally they became abandoned, and their repair and preservation neglected. They were useless for any other purpose, and since stone of which they were constructed, could not be utilized for anything else, they were allowed to remain. The Nile Valley at all times being subject to sand storms blowing off from the desert spots, in all directions, here and there exposed at short distances away, the massive masonry of their walls and columns at an early day caught the sand as a prairie shed would drifting snow, and banked it up. Unlike snow, however, it was indestructible, and, instead of melting, would harden by the overflowing Nile from time to time. No one cared to undertake the job (as would be expected in so poor a country) of clearing the sand and mud away. It necessarily soon became of such immensity and solidity, that, even modern enterprise and means have hesitated long at the enormous expense involved in clearing the rubbish away, much of which to this day remains. In the absence of any other explanation made or attempted, so far as my researches go, I offer this as a reasonable one, at least.

Why the temples and monuments became lost to the world for many centuries.

Thebes, once inhabited by 4,000,000 now a beautiful plain.

When standing upon the east bank of the Nile, and looking west from Luxor, we see before us the old site of Thebes, once the mightiest city of the world, now nothing but a beautiful plain.

[17]

A glance further north, out upon the old historic ground, the crumbled pile of rock and stone which, at a distance seems like a small mountain spur, with its long lines of walls, is the Ramesseum, erected by the proudest of the Pharaohs, Rameses II, to serve as the greatest memorial of his fame and glory. Beyond the structures and some distance therefrom, rise two great colossi from the green valley, which, viewed in the morning from a point far away, seem like massive Gods in granite, sitting at ease upon the velvet lawn of a beautiful garden, communing in silence with the rising sun, invoking the favor of that great orb. Still further north are seen the colonnades, capped with papyrus buds, which adorn the front of the ancient temple of Seti I, founded in honor of Ammon, which, with its sharply defined walls, and hoary parts crumbling into mere relics here and there, seems like a grim old visage standing alone, battling with the elements of time, through the struggle of over three thousand years. It has bravely and marvelously combatted its foe— whose final conquest, before long, is becoming painfully apparent.

The great Colossi loom up like massive gods.

Turning from this and looking west, we see at the very base of the Lybian mountains and resting against its precipitous side, the temple of Deir el Bahari, which, with its long line of columns in front and at the sides of its terraces at its entrance,—if approached from a lower level below,—is a suggestion of a modern capitol edifice, with its red sandstone glittering in the light

Temple of Deirel-Bahari on mountain side looks grand.

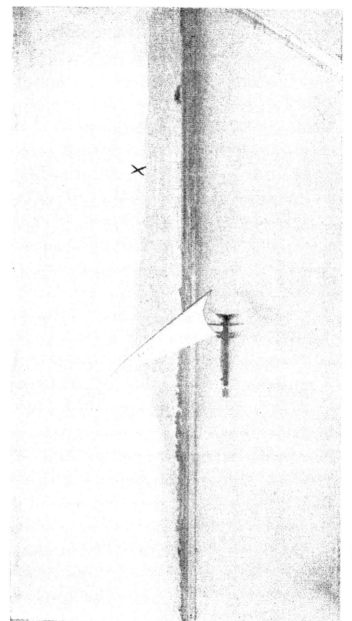

View from Luxor across the Nile where Tombs are located, indicated by X (opposite)

of the morning sun, and built by Queen Hat-shepsowet three thousand four hundred years ago, as a monument to her glory while ruling as Regent for her brother Thutmosis III.

There are to be seen the lesser temples, and in the mountain side, innumerable caves like swallow holes in a sand bank, where princes of the royal families, and high priests of Thebes were buried, affirming the presence of a great Necropolis here, whose mummies at Cairo tell their history, to say nothing of the great tombs of the illustrious kings and queens, found in the valley of the Libyan range, out of sight from the Nile, and but a short distance therefrom.

Having now taken a distant view of the picture described, which lies before you from the east bank of the Nile at Luxor like a panoramic scene, we proceed across the plain and inspect more closely the details, and what then do we find?

We discover so much of indisputable history, *Absolutely indisputable history.* beautiful architecture, painting, sculpturing, buildings, mysterious mechanical productions, so many pagan Gods, illustrations of domestic life, warfare, victories, territorial conquests, religious worship, offerings, gloomy conceptions of death; so much of art in the manufacture of jewelry and utensils, wondrous skill in the mummification of the human body, so much self glorification as well as glorification of animals, all depicted upon and as strongly engraven in stone in every temple and tomb as though executed but yesterday, that we do not know where to begin

[19]

to tell the story or to end the tale. These temples, have slumbered silently for about twenty centuries beneath the mud and sand of the Nile, heaped up by the winds of the Lybian desert. These tombs were secretly built and filled in to evade the robber's spoil for all time, when the mortal remains of their Imperial occupants entered their portals for final rest. Their translatable inscriptions, chiseled deeply in stone and granite, all together form a book of history absolutely incontestable and irrefutable of contemporaneous life as well as prehistoric events. The thought of their unquestioned authenticity and knowledge of their undebatable character, impossible of impeachment or contradiction, should always be uppermost in the mind, in order to disabuse it of the very natural skepticism concerning the accuracy of history involving, in the dim vista, events preceding the birth of Christ two thousand or more years. The thought that we see the same sun, moon and stars, the same river and mountains, that are here now, as did the sons of Ham, or others who first inhabited this land, no matter whether four thousand or ten thousand years ago, we can readily understand and believe, and this without the slightest tinge of incredulity; but, one accustomed to learn ancient history from books, writings or legends, with their destructible and fragile character, being copies, or translations, of unauthenticated originals, do not generally impress the mind satisfactorily. More particularly is it so when such history is based on popular tradition, which necessarily lacks testimonial force. Of course, it is true, that in the Vatican and among the archives of older nations, can be found original, historic information, of contemporaneous events occurring a few years before Christ, but they are so *limited* in scope or comparatively modern in inscription, or inaccessible to the world and few in number, that they do not convince us or furnish a real original picture of antiquity. Hence, we have grown to look upon the far distant past, that is, events preceding the Roman Empire, or the civilization of Europe, as matters of such uncertainty that events, like its lost arts, cannot be determined satisfactorily, and are so deeply buried in the sea of oblivion that there is no hope of light being thrown upon them. Not so here—the temples, pyramidal and rock tombs of Egypt everywhere are opening to the whole world their books of contemporaneous history, over a range of from one thousand to four thousand years before Christ; unfolded by the spade and read by the light of the *Rosetta* stone and other means so simple, that the language of the hieroglyphics has become a modernized tongue. Perhaps right here it is well to give a brief account of what the *Rosetta* stone is, and how it affords a key to the hieroglyphics which was a dead language for more than twenty centuries after Christ.

By Rosetta stone hieroglyphics have become a modernized tongue.

It may be remarked that the earlier Greeks and Romans, successors to the ancient Egyptians, had but little if any interest in the language of other nations. They also, as is well known, had no special linguists which would acquaint their people with foreign languages. As a result, nothing could be learned from them except that the Egyptians had several kinds of writing used for different purposes, and that one, if not two, of these, was confined to sacred uses. It is well known also that their accounts and the information that they gave of the Egyptian life and language, as well as institutions, were *very generally erroneous*. In this way the language of the ancient Egyptians, after the conquest of it by foreign nations, fell into *disuse* and became dead and unknown to the world for practically over twenty centuries. It happened that one of

Napoleon formed Key to Egyptian history in his Egyptian campaign.

Napoleon's engineers, in 1799, one M. Broussard, dug up at a place called Rosetta, near the Mediterranean, a black slab of stone, containing only a very few square feet, with an inscription in hieroglyphics, also in the Demotic and the Greek languages. By this a text was discovered of which the Greek version stated that it was an ascription of divine honors to one of the Ptolemies, and that the hieroglyphic and Demotic versions were transcriptions of the Greek text. In this way that which had been a dead language over such a vast vista of time was revived and given light, so that expert Egyptologists can read the inscriptions engraven upon the temples and in the tombs with the same facility and accuracy of interpretation as they can the Hebrew or the Latin languages.

This stone is now in the British Museum.

[22]

Interest deepens in the revelations of the past, which these recently unearthed monuments of former antiquity present, as the prodigious volume of history, engraven and painted thereon in the language of the ancient Egyptians, the meaning of which has now been made plain by means of the Rosetta stone, becomes apparent. The quantity and multiplicity of the inscriptions in the tombs, as well as on the temples, are so amazingly great, that the extent thereof only gradually becomes fully appreciated after one carefully surveys the field and closely studies the details. At the outset, it is a grave mistake to suppose that we find *only* a *few* old ruins here and there, that are dumb and mute, like those of Rome or Athens, speaking no language, voicing to us no history. We must realize, in order to excite our deepest interest, the great fact that, instead of having before us only a few crumbling monuments of its past, of inferior dimensions, we have many of them—not less than two hundred and fifty—minutely described by the guide books, and most of which are of great size, and many in a marvelous state of preservation, all blazing forth with hieroglyphical light, proclaiming in relief, engraving or painting, the life and sentiment of a great people, which, though largely pagan, nevertheless human and real. Take, for instance, the great temple at Luxor. By actual measurement, made by myself, of the hieroglyphics upon its walls, ceilings and colonnades, I found it would require a ribbon two feet in width, about nineteen miles and one-half long,

Number of chiseled inscriptions on temples and tombs amazingly great and clear.

19½ *miles of hieroglyphic history on one temple alone at Luxor.*

upon which to reproduce the hieroglyphics alone in this one great temple. This result was arrived at by approximating a fair average, allowing for some figure hieroglyphics several feet in height and dimensions, while in others, six to eight inches, mostly vertical and three or four inches apart. Now, when it was considered that there are at least a dozen great temples and tombs in which solid hieroglyphical inscriptions are engraved and written, we can at this day even read, in its temples and tombs alone, hundreds of miles of hieroglyphics relating important events occurring many thousand years ago in the social, political, military, commercial, artistic and religious life of the nation.

These tombs and temples referred to are on the site of the ancient City of Thebes, one containing a population said to be over 4,000,000, and now nothing but a vast farming plain, upon which the mud huts of the Arabs, and not many of them, together with these old temples, mark the place where it formerly stood.

Tomb of Amenophis II, only one at present time in which a Pharaoh has been found and left in its original Sarcophagus. Died 1515 years ago.

Photographed by the Author, copyright 1909.

CHAPTER III

The Great Tomb of Amenophis II, with the Pharaoh Himself Therein on Exhibition in a Mountainside

TO me even more interesting than the temples now unearthed, with all their hundreds of acres of area, which they now cover, are the rock tombs of the Pharaohs, in Biban-Mulak, the old necropolis, and the real Westminster of Thebes. Take, for instance, the tomb of *Amenophis II,* erected about 1,500 years B. C., and what do we find in it, as typical of many others in the immediate vicinity? This is it: After winding our way over the great plain of Thebes, which has the argricultural aspects of rich, alluvial land, fresh with green crops, around through the narrow paths several miles away from the west bank of the Nile, we come to a narrow path, in the Lybian range of mountains. They loom up high and strong, running north and south several miles from the river's bank, and which range extends several hundred miles, presenting the appearance, as seen from Luxor, of a great, precipitous and quite regularly sky-lined ridge of mountain spurs. We now come to a short valley, a picture of which is herewith presented, appearing to be not over five hundred feet in width nor half a mile in length, upon all sides of which, excepting the one through which we enter, great limestone mountains (treeless, herbless) piercing the blue vault of heaven as you look upward. There is no place on earth where the sky appears bluer than at this very spot, in contrast with the limestone mountains and precipices that tower above your head. In fact, it is the remark of everyone that the sky can be hardly said to be blue, because of its intensity of color, but more resembles black. Passing on, we find bored into the face of the mountain a great tunnel, ten or twelve feet in diameter, with steps in regular proportion, extending about forty-five degrees right angle, for several hundred feet in a tortuous way, in solid rock, until you finally come to two or more chambers. The first of these chambers approximates about thirty feet square, with a ceiling about fifteen feet in height. Immediately adjoining this chamber, and having the same roof, is another room of a so-called crypt, the floor of which is several feet lower than the first chamber. In this crypt we find a beautiful rose-colored sarcophagus, weighing many tons, polished like a piano with such brilliancy that you can nearly see your face in it. The *dados* and *friezes* of the chambers are painted beautifully with variegated colors. The friezes are the Lotus flower of Egypt, which flowers, like the

The mountain where tombs concealed, are treeless, grassless and herbless.

Tomb of Amenophis II most beautiful. Discovered in 1898 by Loret.

[26]

Pharaohs, have long since passed from earthly existence. The ceiling is painted in a beautiful blue sky color and dotted with golden stars. Upon the walls and pillars are painted in bright colors, Gods of the entombed Pharaoh. He is Amenophis II, who died and was buried 1,420 years before the birth of our Saviour. In the sarcophagus is found the Pharaoh himself, wrapped in his royal bandages, with feet, hands and head exposed, lying precisely as he was put there by the high priests of Ammon. So well preserved is his body that his features are perfect, his teeth slightly protruding in such a way as to show that the art of dentistry was practiced upon him. His hair is upon his head; his hands are almost of the normal size, with finger nails well manicured, upon the tips of which is found the brownish liquid which even to this very day ornaments the nails of Egyptians. In truth, as he lies there, he looks like a man just having died, beneath the electric light which is hung from the ceiling above in such manner as to throw a sombre hue upon his face, imparting a wonderfully natural appearance. This light has been introduced by the Government in recent years. There is hardly a scratch anywhere to be seen on the walls or ceilings. The bright electric lights illuminate the chambers and exhibit the original colors with much beauty; in fact, there is nothing needed to give it the elegance of a modern royal mausoleum. The Pharaoh who preceded Menephtah of the Exodus by about two hundred years, lies in the

Teeth, hair and features of Pharaoh perfect.

Bright electric lights illuminate the Royal Chamber where the Pharaoh lies in State.

same state to-day, in a finer tomb than many European monarchs buried in the last century. People of all nations pass by his bier, in reverent mood, in one continuous procession, paying in silence their respects to the dead monarch. They lean forth with curious glances, and look down upon that face with the same sense of nearness as though he died but yesterday. Strange this turn in the fame of Amenophis II. He was buried thirty-three hundred and forty-three years ago, and fourteen hundred and twenty years before Christ, and centuries before Europe was civilized. Now, in the glare of the twentieth century civilization, his tomb is unlocked and the world invited to come and view his remains lying in state, carefully preserved and tenderly guarded. The world has accepted the invitation. Kings and Queens, Princes and Princesses, from all over the world, call at his tomb and pay their homage to a dead sovereign of their own rank, and lay upon his sarcophagus a garland of flowers such as was placed upon his breast in the ceremony of his burial, which now is seen beneath the plate glass, resting upon his body as originally deposited. Not only sovereigns of the earth come hither to pay their respects to him, but mankind of all classes wend their way from all countries to the tomb, in order that they, too, may look upon him. Indeed, we think that Amenophis II is having the greatest funeral procession viewing his remains, and of greater distinction, than any with which a human monarch was ever honored. The doc-

Body of the dead Pharaoh lies in state, viewed by the world.

All sovereigns on earth come and lay flowers on the Pharaohs' caskets.

Tomb of Amenophis II. only one at present time in which
a Pharaoh has been found and left in his original
Sarcophagus. Died 3343 years ago

trine of the "Book of the Dead," extracts of which are written above his sarcophagus proclaiming the return of life after death, strong in the faith in which he died, seems almost exemplified by this recent part which his hoary locks and physical being are playing in the human affairs of the day. If at least his *soul* has not returned to this world after slumbering thirty-three hundred and forty-three years, his *body* has.

This tomb of Amenophis II, which was discovered twenty-five years ago under the auspices of the French Government, by Loret, contained a side chamber, or recess, where nine other royal bodies were found, most of whom were well preserved and absolutely identified by their imperial robes in which they were wrapped and the cartouches upon their coffins.

In a side chamber of the Sepulcher, slumbered nine Pharaohs over thirty centuries.

CHAPTER IV

*An Humble Arab, Rassul, in 1875
Found the First Pharaoh's Tomb and
Contents in Thirty-one Centuries,
with Seven Pharaohs, Including
Rameses the Great*

GREAT as was the discovery of the Amenophis II tomb, in 1898, there was one still greater and far more important in the value of its contents, found intact, and the greatest in all the history of the world of which there is any record. That was the so-called RASSUL tomb, found in the base of the same mountain only a few feet away, in 1875, and kept by its discoverer a secret for six years, when its contents were taken out by the Egyptian officials and placed in the Museum at Cairo.

The discovery of tomb facinating tale of romance and drama.

Now, here hangs a tale of romance, more picturesque and exciting than any ever written in fiction or history. That of "Robinson Crusoe" and those of "The Arabian Nights" excite the interest of both old and young, although they are purely fictitious, and rank, as they do, among the

ABD-ER RASSUL

The Theban Cave Dweller, discoverer of the greatest of all Tombs containing *Mummies of the Pharaohs of the Bible*, including RAMESES the Great

most fascinating in literature; but, if those tales *excite* the interest, the story of Rassul and his discovery *rivets* the interest of mankind, both old and young, so irresistibly that both "Robinson Crusoe" and "The Arabian Nights" are eclipsed in the fascination of a real and almost unbelievable recital of this drama.

On the adjoining page is the only known picture ever taken of Abd-er-Rassul, the humble Arab who found the key which opened the first tomb of the Pharaohs, with its contents, locked from the world for over thirty-one hundred years.

The romance of this picturesque but simple dweller upon the Theban Plain at Luxor far surpasses in human interest anything in "The Arabian Nights," since the characters there were *imaginary*—here the hero is *real*. He it was who, in 1875, discovered, amidst the hundreds of thousands of tons of fine disintegrated rock, now and then a small *granite chip,* which, on very close inspection, revealed the slightest mark of a cutting instrument, to his discriminating eye, but which to others was wholly oblivious, or meaningless. For more than thirty centuries this tremendous pile of fine sand and granite stone had tumbled down from the bald cliffs of the Libyan Mountain above, upon the long-forgotten Necropolis of ancient Thebes. To the keen eye of old Rassul the cut chips seemed more like the work of man than the hand of *Allah.* He saw in these occasional cut sands a trail which might lead to gilded tombs and

Small cut chips looking like sand gave Rassul a clue to his great discovery.

jeweled treasures of the Pharaohs for which the world had searched in vain thirty centuries. Working secretly alone, except with a brother, did this cunning Arab dig for many long, dreary years in the dead silence of the night amidst the sombre shadows of the great cliffs where he toiled. He went down deeper and deeper, and yet, here and there, wherever the trail of the cut particles led him, he followed. After a while, and many feet below the debris, he came to an underground corridor, leading to a tomb full of Pharaohs, and found more than six car-loads of priceless funerary articles, rivaling, if not surpassing, in beauty, brilliancy, elegance and value, those which are now found in the tomb of Tut-ankh-Amen, and all, or most of which, are now on exhibition at the Cairo Museum. In this tomb were found Rameses the Great, mightiest of all Pharaohs, known as the Pharaoh of the Bondage; Seti I, father of Rameses the Great, and, next to his son, the most famous of all Egyptian monarchs; Amenophis I, Thutmosis III, ranking next to the Rameses in glory, and other Pharaohs resting together in gilded coffins, within a chamber of imperial splendor.

Rassul concealed his great discovery for six years from all the world.

With grim silence did this cunning Arab conceal his great find, and for six years thereafter. On that occasion no wireless flashed the event to the four corners of the world. Not even the Arabs of the nearby village where he lived knew of it, such was his masterly concealment. He was but a poor man. He lived like the beasts of the desert, sheltered in a cave at El Kurnah, near his newly found treasures, less than a mile away.

Since the contents of the tomb had been concealed from, and abandoned by the world for over thirty-one centuries, Rassul pondered much as to whether by the moral Law of Moses, the Koran of Mohammed, or the Law of Egypt, these treasures should not belong to him. He reasoned that a claim of title thereto could not be established by the decendants or heirs of the Pharaohs, to whom the contents belonged originally, because there were no descendants or heirs; neither were the priceless contents within the category of minerals in the earth over which sovereigns claimed dominion by the Law of Nations. To whom then did they belong, asked Rassul of himself? He thought, and perhaps rightly, too, that he was the owner of these treasures by right of discovery—at least he did not risk a chance of losing the same by taking legal advice. So it came to pass that he must find a partner, who could help him to dispose of the precious articles in his underground warehouse, to the portals of which he, and he alone, could enter. He knew that a traveler coming through the land would not credit his title as genuine to anything he might offer for sale, other than a basket of eggs, or a peck of corn, for his humble station in life would excite suspicion if he claimed to own anything more valuable. So he tactfully confided in the English and Belgian Consul at Luxor, *Mustapha Pasha*, he of rather easy virtue, but robed with

Before long, Rassul found partner to help dispose of his royal warehouse of precious treasures.

[33]

the prestige of an *official* representative. With him he bargained for a division of the spoils Wisely, however, did he conceal even from Mustapha the hiding place of his treasures. Soon wealthy tourists, travelers up the Nile, were approached secretly and prevailed upon to buy now and then immensely valuable, if not priceless, articles, consisting of scarabi, papyri, and other objects now in the British and other world museums, for small prices. Of course, with the O. K. of Mustapha, there was neither fraud nor want of good title, thought they. Maspero, Director General of Antiquities at Cairo, hearing of what appeared to him the dreamiest of Pharaoh tales (*for until now no royal tomb with its contents had been discovered in over thirty centuries*), started an official investigation, and found the owner, who brought the articles to his partner, Mustapha, for sale. *It was Abd-er-Rassul.* He found him one morning in his humble cave near the fringe of the Theban Plain, at the base of the mountain opposite Luxor. He was arrested and taken to Kena, the capitol of the province where he lived, and in due form of law, imprisoned for several months, all of which there is a court record. He was adamant against all attempts of the officials to extract from him any statement which would lead them to find where his warehouse was. He grimly closed his mouth, so strong was he in his faith that it was none of their business, according to the law of England or of Egypt. Although all sorts of criminal punishment were threatened, and physi-

Rassul found a partner to sell his wares.

There is a court record of his romance.

cal pain and torment as well, if he should persist in his refusal to disclose his secret, he stolidly held out for two months, and then was set free. He could not be *forced* to tell where his friends, Rameses the Great, Seti I, and half a dozen others of his companion Pharaohs, were hidden, yet he could be *bribed* to do so. So, it came further to pass that the offer of fifty pounds a year and a house to live in for life, softened him and he was thereby made willing to hand his old friends over to the Egyptian officials and surrender his claim of right and title to their imperial belongings. It must be borne in mind that before his disclosure and the bargain he made with the officials, he possessed this warehouse of royal bodies and several carloads of their personal articles for six years after he made his discovery and kept it all to himself. The articles being bulky, most of them he could not well take from their hiding place without some of his fellow Arabs learning about it and where they came from. So, when he saw before him the vision of a house and fifty pounds a year, he imagined that to be of more value to him than to persist in his claim of right to the contents he had discovered, and yielded to the temptation of accepting the offer. An incident happened, however, which quickly induced him to thus decide. A younger brother had learned about the tomb, and he, too, began to secretly lug things away in the dark without Ab's consent or knowledge, and to pocket the whole of the proceeds without recognizing that his brother

Rassul, at last, for a house and $250 a year for life sold his warehouse, and gave up the secret.

had any right thereto or any part thereof. Immediately on learning of this, he went to Kena and there bargained at once for the disclosure and his pension. Immediately thereafter, under his guidance, the Egyptian officials, led by him, prowled about on the 5th day of July, 1881, among the desolate mounds of the old Theban Necropolis, way up in the side of the mountain, over 100 feet above the plain of Thebes below.

Rassul was the modern "Moses" who led the officials through wilderness of mystery to the Pharaohs.

With the light of torches did they follow breathlessly their modern "Moses," who led them in the dark wilderness of mystery to a carload of Pharaohs and six carloads of imperial belongings, where they had slept for over three thousand years.

Learning of the leading part Abd-er-Rassul had in the world's long struggle to find the royal tombs of Egypt, with their contents, and while stopping at the time at Luxor for several weeks in the winter of 1908, I looked him up. I sent for him with a guide who could speak his language. He came to me with the guide I selected, and through him, from his own lips, I learned the above story as I have given it to you, the main facts of which are verified in the official guide of the Egyptian National Museum. He seemed about 83 years of age, although he claimed he was some younger. He was intelligent, and had that bright, fascinating twinkle of the eye for which the cunning Arabs are famous. He was very shy. His white turban upon his head, white whiskers, and flowing black gown which he wore, and tall figure, gave him a

Rassul posed but once for his picture and that is presented herewith.

truly romantic and patriarchal appearance as he was relating to me the great story. I asked him if he ever had a photograph taken of himself, and he said he had not. I then asked him for the privilege of taking his photograph, and he at first hesitated, fearing that it possibly meant either another imprisonment or physical harm to his body. On assuring him that it meant neither, and that I desired it to take home with me to America for the purpose of remembering and introducing him to my friends, he consented. This is the first photograph for which he ever posed, and the last, for he soon thereafter died. I thought that Abd-er-Rassul, by serving two months behind the bars, had paid even a small price for the transcendent glory of being the pioneer discoverer of Pharaoh's tomb with its contents, which had been lost to the world for over thirty centuries, and the only and first tomb of that kind. He is now introduced to the world for the first time as the star actor in the modern Theban drama, with his accompanying picture. His discovery of the first tomb with its priceless contents, together with the key of a *cut chip,* leading thereto, which he gave to subsequent discoverers, gives him a prior claim to fame over Lord Carnarvon for the discovery lately of the sepulchre of Tut-ankh-Amen.

Taking Rassul's photograph.

Rassul star actor in modern Theban drama.

Our hero was the pioneer discoverer of a Pharaoh's tomb containing its priceless contents and royal bodies, the greatest found or perhaps that ever will be in point of historic interest. The success of Rassul was not achieved by wealth, aided by experience, as was the recent tomb of Tut-ankh-Amen, but accomplished only by his native instinct. This he undoubtedly inherited from his robber ancestors, who so skillfully raided the royal sepulchres at Thebes, at the commencement of the new Empire, over three thousand one hundred years ago, as to make it necessary that the sovereigns and high priests at that period should bore into the mountainside, the tomb which Rassul discovered, in order to evade further depredation upon the bodies of their great Monarchs and their imperial belongings. This tomb had been submerged, it must be remembered, deep down into the disintegrated rock and sand for over thirty-one hundred years, and that all traces of it had been lost to the world for that great period of time, as much so as the sepulchre of Moses, or Aaron, or Joseph, or Solomon, or Abraham, have been unknown and forgotten long before the birth of Christ. It was closed and unknown to all the world even

Ceaser and Alexander tried to find the old Pharaohs, but did not succeed.

before Caesar lived and conquered Egypt, or Alexander swept over victoriously the plains of the Nile with his arms and put Egypt under his subjection. It is said of them that they looked and dug in vain for the great prize and failed. Napoleon, as late as 1797, when he overran Egypt with his victorious army, slaughtering 15,000 Mamelukes at the base of the great pyramid, brought with him 100 savants, the most skilled scientists in France. Under the master mind of their great conqueror they toiled hard in order to, but could not, find a single trace of

[38]

a Pharaoh's tomb with its contents. The nearest that Napoleon came to it was his great discovery of the Rosetta stone, to which we have already alluded, but this did not give more to him than a key to the hieroglyphic history of Egypt. It did not tell him where to find the bodies, gilded thrones, or jeweled sceptres of the Pharaohs, or builders of the mighty monuments and temples, relics of a past glory which blazon forth the highest in all the annals of mankind. These great conquerors, Caesar, Alexander and Napoleon, looked upon the monuments and great temples of Egypt with a worshipful admiration; but even they knew not how or where to find their builders, although they knew of their history. These great rulers of the world, that is to say, Caesar and Alexander, looked back even in their day upon the glory of the Pharaohs for many centuries before them, and which inspired their own ambition. They thought so far back, as even in their day, that the bodies and every material trace of them and their burial belongings, like those of the biblical characters in the Old Testament, had long since crumbled into dust and their sepulchers with them, never again to be resurrected. To them the task of finding these priceless treasures was seemingly a hopeless one. The personal history of the Pharaohs for twenty-five centuries or more had been a blank, that had gone up and evaporated into space, with the smoke that belched forth from the fire of the Alexandrian library, several centuries before Christ, if, indeed, that history

Caesar and Alexander conquered Egypt, but could not find Pharaohs in tombs.

Before Rosetta stone found, history of Pharaohs disappeared in smoke with Alexandrian library, B. C.

had not been lost to mankind long before then. The only history remaining was misty and uncertain, as found in the Biblical accounts, and limited then only to a very few isolated incidents of life. They spoke only hazily of some acts of glory and deeds of oppression in the most general way. Nothing was authentic, until the Rosetta stone unfolded the history of Egypt and its rulers for over forty centuries by affording the key of interpretation to the hieroglyphic language. As we have shown, this history was engraven on its myriad temple walls and forest of broken pillars everywhere looming up on the Theban plains, amidst the most extensive and tremendous ruins on earth. This great discovery by Napoleon only threw light upon dynasties, but did not find royal chariots; it gave accounts of conquerors and conquests, but did not capture their sceptres or thrones. The Rosetta stone, while it led to the discovery of the day of the birth and death of the ancient sovereigns of the land and the diseases which killed them, it did not find their sepulchres. These were as grimly and securely concealed from the world by the priests of the new Empire, over three thousand years ago, as rocks lodged half a mile in a mountain side. May we not well ask then, who, of all the myriads of men, both high and low, some for spoil, others for glory, for over thirty centuries searched for the bodies of the Pharaohs and their treasures, was it that first opened a Pharaoh's mausoleum with its contents intact? Amidst the great commotion which has within the last two months again set fire to the world's enthusiasm over the discovery of Tut-ankh-Amen's tomb, it is proper to pause one moment and ask who was it that first opened such a royal sepulchre of the Pharaohs with its contents, and when? Since the rise of the new Empire, thirty-one hundred years ago, there was a time, of course, and a place, when such discovery was made. As we have shown, the place was the Theban Necropolis, the time was 1875, and the discoverer no less than Abd-er-Rassul, whom we have introduced to the world as certainly the star actor upon the stage of the modern Theban drama.

Adb-er-Rassul has long since died. In life he discovered the *bodies* of Rameses and Seti, but could not find their *souls*. Now, since he has himself taken flight to spiritland, from which bourne no traveler has ever returned, he may have discovered also the spirits of those great Monarchs. By the Law of Nature he cannot turn them over to us, as he did their bodies. The fame which attaches to him for what he did becomes all the more apparent as time passes. The credit given him at the time, and for a long while thereafter, was indeed very meagre, but the world, however, is beginning to look upon him in his true light and to accord him the credit which is his just due.

The recent world-wide excitement and enthusiasm over the discovery of the tomb of Tut-ankh-Amen, causing the public press, magazines and periodicals of all countries to blazon forth praises to Lord Carnarvon for his recent triumph in the discovery of a Pharaoh's tomb with its precious belongings, have turned attention to Rassul by those few who know of him.

As an illustration of this we might mention in passing that, during the month of this writing, several cable despatches have come from Luxor to the American press, representing that the descendants of the humble Rassul are being much sought after and interviewed, because of the fame justly due their ancestor, as the pioneer discoverer of a Pharaoh's tomb with its royal occupants and its contents, the greatest of all.

It might be well now to give some further details of this great Pharaohonic mausoleum and the disposition of its contents.

Place marked X where Rassul discovered Tomb with carload
of Pharaohs including RAMESES, THE GREAT

CHAPTER V

Disposition Made of the Contents of the Tomb After Rassul Surrendered His Claim Thereto and Turned It Over to the Government

IT was on Wednesday, July 5, 1881, that Emile Brugsch Pasha, then sub-Conservator of the Cairo Museum, accompanied by Effendi Kamal, secretary and interpreter at the Museum, and Tadrus Moutafian, inspector of the Pyramid district, were conducted to the tomb by Rassul, pursuant to his bargain made with the Government that he should be paid a pension for showing them the hiding place of the Pharaohs, which he claimed he owned, or of which, at least, he had possession for six years, with a key to its portal.

Between el-Assassif and the Valley of the Queens, the chain of hills which separates the Bab-el-Moluk from the Theban plains, forms a series of natural amphitheatres, the best known of which is the famous Temple of Dier-el-Bahari. There is a knoll called Sheikh Abd-el-

Gurnah, a little farther on, which is about one hundred and eighty feet above the level of the cultivated land below. It was behind this knoll, and quite in the base of the mountain, where this subterranean mausoleum was found. Here it was that the high priests of Ammon had dug a shaft to the depth of about thirty-four feet and about six feet in width. At the bottom of it, in the west wall, was the entrance to a gallery which measured about four feet and a half in width and about five feet in height. After running about twenty-four feet it turned abruptly to the north and continued about one hundred and eight feet farther into solid rock. This gallery finally terminated in an irregularly oblong-shaped chamber about twenty-five feet in length. Scattered on the floor beside the coffins were innumerable boxes such as are now being found in the tomb of Tut-ankh-Amen, filled with funerary statuettes, bronze libation vases, canopic jars and various other articles, including royal funeral tents. All along the gallery there was great disorder. The official report of the entrance made at the time states that the advance had to be made on all fours, with the dim light of candles, led by Rassul, without any certainty as to where feet and hands should be placed, so heaped up and confused were the contents. The coffins and bodies rapidly scanned by the light of the candle, were found to bear historic names, such as Rameses the Great, his father, Seti I; Amenophis I, Thutmosis II, his son, Thutmosis III; Rameses II; Siamanu, Saqnunri, Ahmosis,

Queen Ahhotpu, and many others. There were besides these August Monarchs, mummified bodies of the royal families, consisting of Princes and Princesses, there being all told thirty-seven, besides six carloads of funerary and household articles. The confusion was at its height in the chamber when these officials learned that they had unearthed a tomb full of Pharaohs, among whom there were the greatest Kings and conquerors the world had ever known.

37 royal bodies intact found, including seven Pharaohs and members of the families in Rassul tomb.

The Museum steamboat, which had been hastily summoned, soon arrived five miles away at Luxor on the Nile. To transport back to Cairo the royal freight, forty-eight hours of hard work were required to take out of the tomb its contents, and several hours to convey them from the sepulchre to the river bank. At last, on the 14th day of July, the royal bodies and their coffins, carefully wrapped in sheets and properly protected, were deposited upon the Museum steamboat, which soon started back, four hundred and twenty miles to Cairo, with its cargo of Kings. As the steamboat proceeded towards Cairo, millions of the populace flocked to the shores of the Nile to witness the unparalleled scene of their ancient sovereigns of thirty centuries ago having been resurrected, and all riding together in an ordinary boat toward another resting place. It is said that the fellahin women followed it uttering loud cries and with their hair disheveled, while the men fired guns, as they do at funerals over there. What a change in the condition of things was it for these great

Pharaohs! Over three thousand years ago they were taken from time to time in stately funeral barges, or other sumptuous vehicles of state, and carried to their final resting place in the rocks of Bab-el-Moluk amidst dazzling pomp and show, not the least of which must have been the great pageant of mourners and priests. Now they were all huddled together as so much freight and taken back over the same old plain in the midst of the same surroundings to the same old Nile, which has kept on flowing incessantly since their day. They were sent in a miserable Arab boat to Cairo, that we of the twentieth century may look upon them and their belongings as did their subjects who mourned their death at that time. It took four years of study, in fact, even before the Museum itself or the world realized what it had secured.

Millions on the Nile witnessed passage of Pharaohs up to Cairo, amidst mournful cries and fire of guns.

The unwrapping of the bodies was begun in the month of May, 1886, and was continued to the last days of June of that year. Scientists and experts were in mortal fear that the exposure of the bodies to the air would cause their immediate disintegration, an impression we are glad to say was not well founded.

Of course, the moment that such a great discovery was made the world evinced much solicitude as to the condition of the bodies concealed within their coverings. Naturally everyone was anxious that the coverings should be removed so that the actual body of the Pharaoh himself who oppressed the world, and Israel in particular, might be looked upon. The world could not understand what the great delay was occasioned by in removing these coverings, except upon the imaginary theory that the experts of the Museum had learned that the bodies had crumbled into dust, and that, therefore, it was deemed wiser to hold the world in suspense concerning the fact as long as possible. Again, this impression was not well founded; there had something happened which held in abeyance the process of official removal of the bandages, which was only known to the officials themselves. It appears that one of the mummies had the outside wrappings taken off from it and while the process was going on it crumbled to pieces. There was hardly time for a photograph to be taken before the body of the mummy resolved itself into dust, losing its form and figure instantly. Under such circumstances and thereafter those in charge of the delicate task properly refrained from unswathing the more important of the Pharaohs. However, being encouraged by the fact that a majority of the bodies could be exposed to the air without risk of immediate extinguishment, with which they had experimented later, it was finally decided to take off the bandages of the great Pharaohs themselves. Thereupon a distinguished coterie of scientific men and officials assembled to witness the removal of the coverings. Among others present were High Commissioners of Great Britain and Turkey, several Ambassadors, the Kedhive of Egypt, and representatives of other nations who dignified the ceremony with their attendance. The coffin and

Why unwrapping of bodies delayed several years.

the outer wrappings indicated the name of the Pharaoh or person whom it enclosed. They first selected the body of Rameses the Great and proceeded to remove his wrappings. After the verification by the officials of the winding sheet being that of the great Monarch, in the presence of all the other illustrious persons, in order that there might never afterwards arise any question as to the identification of the body, the first wrapping was removed. There was found to be a strong cloth rolled all around the body, then a second one, kept in place by being sewed up; next two more thicknesses of small bandages, after which a new winding sheet of strong linen enveloping the whole body. Upon this sheet, curiously enough, they found a figure representing the Goddess Nut, the favorite Goddess of Rameses. This figure was a little less than a yard in length, drawn in two colors, red and white, required by the ritual for the dead adopted by this sovereign. Beneath this was one more bandage, which, when removed, there was nothing remaining except a loose piece of linen. On this was some sort of spots, supposed to be matter used in the mummification of the body. *It now became quite evident that Rameses the Great was near at hand.* One can easily imagine how curious, solicitous, solemn and reverential the distinguished guests became at this point. It is unfortunate that the moving picture process prevailing at this day and now at hand at the tomb of Tut-ankh-Amen was not there. Finally, and at the moment of greatest suspense, the op-

August assemblage of distinguished men witness scene of unwrapping of Rameses the Great.

[48]

erator in charge delicately lifted the last layer of linen from his body, and when done there lay before that august assemblage upon his bier the body intact of the most powerful and illustrious Monarch the world has ever known, Rameses the Great. There is presented with this sketch the reproduction of a photograph taken of his head at the time. As is seen thereby, his head is long, the top of the skull is quite bare; that his hair is quite thick; the locks of his hair were white at the time of his death, colored a little by spices used in embalment. His eyebrows are large and white, while his eyes are quite small and close together. He had a low and very narrow forehead; a long nose, very much arched, and what we would call a Roman nose; cheek bones very prominent. His ears stand far out from the head, and are pierced from the wearing of earrings. His chin was very prominent, with a strong jaw; thick lipped, with a small mouth. His teeth are excellently preserved, beautifully white. They show wear, as becoming one of his age. His mustache and beard appear very thin, and probably were allowed to grow slightly during is last illness, or they may have grown somewhat after his death. The hairs are white, like those of the head and eyebrows, and a tenth of an inch in length. His skin is brownish, some wrinkled. The face of the Pharaoh is a good likeness of himself in life. The expression is not at all intelligent, but inclines much to that of the animal. But, as a writer of distinction says, "There is to be seen

Detailed description of how Rameses, the Great looks with his hair, teeth and all.

in it an air of sovereign majesty, of resolve and of pride." In consequence of the reduction of the tissues about the neck it is less natural than any part of the entire body. The body is that of an old man, vigorous and robust.

We could go on and enumerate the procedure whereby the Cairo scientists for years carefully unwrapped the other Kings found in the Rassul tomb, including that of Seti I, and Thutmosis III, besides several other illustrious sovereigns found in the tomb reigning in the 18th, 19th, 20th and 21st dynasties, but to do so might become a burdensome repetition. The one already given will fairly serve to furnish the casual reader with the manner in which those in charge looked after and cared for the preservation of these priceless treasures for the benefit and edification of the world.

What we have said concerning the character of the Pharaohs is only for the purpose, not of giving a history of their conquests and their power, but simply to make clear the great value of the contents found in the Rassul tomb, and the importance which that discovery had in stimulating the world in making further searches for prizes of equal value in the Necropolis at Thebes.

Following discovery of Rassul tomb in 1881, was the Loret tomb, 1898, and now that of Carnarvon.

As we have shown in a previous chapter, it was followed by the subsequent discovery, under the auspices of the French Government, by Loret, of the tomb of Amenophis II, in which that Monarch was found with several others, including Menephtah, the Pharaoh of the Exodus, who succeeded Rameses the Great. After the discovery of the Rassul tomb, in 1881, Egyptologists and scientists, backed up by the wealth of many distinguished persons, and governments, prominent among which is that of Mr. Theodore M. Davis, of the United States, have spent vast sums of money in the exploration and excavation in the Theban Necropolis. In this are included the Valley of the Queens, at the base of the east side of the Lybian Mountain, where the Rassul tomb was discovered; at Dier-el-Bahari, and that of the Valley of the Kings, on the west side of the mountain, where the Loret tomb was discovered. But little progress is necessarily made in finding the great prizes, because it takes a vast amount of deep digging over great space under adverse circumstances.

After the expenditure sometimes of years of time and great sums of money, the operation is given up in the hopeless task of finding a great prize and is abandoned without reward.

CHAPTER VI

The Pharaohs Found in the Great Rassul Tomb and the High Lights of Their History

THE Pharaohs found in the tomb discovered by Rassul were, among others, *Rameses I, Rameses II, Rameses III, Seti I, Amenophis I, Thutmosis II and Thutmosis III.*

Rameses I died 1313 B. C. at Thebes. History shows his principal claim to fame to be the fact that he was father of Seti I, grandfather of Rameses II, and founder of the dynasty of Rameses, eleven of whose descendants wielded the kingly sceptre of Egypt. Among the immortal works of glory credited to him on the granite engraven history of his reign was, that he planned and began the vast colonnaded Hall, the world-wide famous Hypostyle Hall of the Temple of Ammon at Karnak, Eastern Thebes, afterwards, however, continued and built by his successors. One who has not seen this wonderful structure cannot realize its great size, or its inexpressibly massive grandeur, even unto this day.

This temple was dedicated to the worship of the God *Ammon*. It consists of great courts, one of which alone is 275 feet deep and 338 feet wide, covering 9,755 square yards. This temple has ever been known as one of the wonders of Egyptian architecture. It rivals the pyramids of Cheops in challenging the admiration of the world as a work of massive grandeur. It covers over twenty acres of land. It has a forest of broken shafts and columns, perhaps none so grand or mighty ever erected by mankind. Within its walls the great Cathedrals of St. Peter at Rome and Notre Dame at Paris could be enclosed and much space left. The roof of the Hypostyle Hall alone is supported by 134 columns, arranged in sixteen rows, with calyx and Bud capitals, on which more than one hundred men can stand without crowding. They are as large as the Trajan column in Rome or the Vendome column in Paris. Many of the columns of the Hall are in a very dilapidated condition; others stand as firm as the day of their erection, most of which are painted and many are exceedingly bright with attractive colors, the lotus flower predominating. This in spite of the fact that thirty centuries have elapsed since their erection, and most of that time they have been buried beneath the sand. They have principally been excavated during the last 100 years. Some parts are still under the process of excavation. The writer has viewed

Temple of Ammon at Thebas rivals the pyramids in massive grandeur.

the ancient Coliseum at Rome and the Acropolis at Athens, both of which are in ruins, at moonlight, and experienced a feeling of fascination and charm seldom before witnessed. He also has viewed the Temple of Ammon at moonlight, amidst the deep shadows cast far and wide by its forests of massive columns and gigantic pylons. A different feeling overtook him there than at the Grecian and Roman ruins. Somehow it was the sense of humility and smallness with which he was irresistibly impressed, mingled with enthusiastic wonder and admiration. We have said humility because, as a being whose existence is supposed to be allotted only the short time of three score years and ten, the conscious comparison of one's short life with this great handiwork of man wrought *thirty-five centuries ago* impresses deeply on him the brevity of our earthly sojourn here; smallness, because you realize you are in the presence of a mighty structure, the dark shadows of which swell its dimensions to almost incomprehensible size in comparison with one's small self.

Rameses II the Caesar or Napoleon of Egypt found.

The fame of *Rameses II* and his character as the greatest of all Pharaohs is well known. He was the *Caesar* of Egypt, reigned as a tyrant in the nineteenth century and died thirty-one hundred and forty-eight years ago, after a rule of sixty-seven years, at the age of about 90. The history of this great sovereign is incomparably better preserved than that either of Caesar or Alexander, and as well authenticated as that of Napoleon. His history is found upon thousands of engraved inscriptions, extending from the Euphrates on the east, America on the west, Europe on the north and Nubia on the south. Statues, carvings and paintings of him are everywhere even *now* to be seen over the vast area of ancient Egypt and its provinces; some, like the giant monolith statue of him prostrate on the sands of Memphis, weighing thousands of tons; there are others, carved high up on the rocks, like that at Abu-Simbel, frowning down upon you from its great height, similar to that of Napoleon at the foot of the Simplon Pass; others decorate temple walls and pylons with hundreds of his engraven and painted portraitures. The priceless shaft of antiquity, most famous one in America, the *Obelisk* in Central Park, even *proclaims his glory*. On it he engraved his name more than thirty-one centuries ago as the ruler of Egypt, and the name of himself is clearly there still. It is seen to-day precisely as he looked upon it with his own proud eyes. London, too, extols him, for there again a great monument of antiquity taken from the sands of Egypt records his kingly sovereignty over that ancient country, engraven by himself.

Rameses name is on Obelisk in Central Park put there over 30 centuries ago.

Besides, his battles, conquests and life are everywhere in hieroglphical history, engraved upon stone and pillar so profusely that, if translated into English, would literally fill several volumes. The geneaology of Washington and his principal deeds are no better authenticated nor more reliable than those of Rameses the Great. He was the tyrant who put to death the first

[55]

born of Israel. He erected vast monuments and mortuary temples, bearing his name to this day, for his own glorification. To do so he brutally enslaved his helpless people at home and the captives brought back in his foreign wars. He was the target at which the Scribes of old and the Prophets in the Bible shot their arrows of censure. So, we have not only inexhaustible hieroglyphic descriptions of his deeds, but frequent Biblical references to the same as well. It was his sister who rescued Moses from the bullrushes. He it was who built canals that connected the Nile with the Red Sea, and which he did for the benefit of his Asiatic possession and better defense of his Empire from Oriental invasion. To find Rameses II in his tomb, with body intact, and bring him back to us after his slumber of thirty-one hundred and forty-eight years, wrapped in the scroll of his history as his shroud, is like a dream, and hardly seems real. Even more strange does it seem than if Caesar or Alexander were resurrected. Even they looked back and thought his body lost to the world for many centuries before their own day and generation.

Rameses' scroll of his history was his burial shroud.

Thutmosis II was a warrior sovereign who fought Nubia and other foreign countries as far as the Euphrates on the east. It was his special custom on return from his campaigns to have triumphal processions in Thebes, parading his captives with imperial pomp and show. He conducted punitive expeditions in Southern Palestine against revolting subjects, and inflicted upon

Thutmosis II found in Rassul tomb.

them great and bloody punishment. The imposing Temple of Hat-Shep-Sut, near the Rassul
tomb, of imposing size and appearance, was used
by him to record his campaigns, where they are
read with much interest.

Thutmosis III, who reigned between 1501 and
1447 B. C., was known as the Obelisk builder,
and otherwise as one of the greatest of Egypt's
Monarchs. He built the Obelisk in our park
which bears his name. At this time Egypt was
at the zenith of its greatness. He was one of
Egypt's most famous Kings. Among his military deeds of great renown was his subjugation
of Syria. During his reign enormous floods of
wealth poured into the kingdom from his foreign
dependencies. Thebes, with its hundred golden
gates, received most of it. Great sums were laid
out by him in the repair and extension of the
Temple of Ammon, to which we have alluded as
one of the architectural and structural wonders
of the world. His sister, Hatshepsut, was co-
regent with him, and shared the honors of his
reign. She was the first great woman in history,
with an aggressive career as a sovereign of
which there is any account. It is not the purpose of this book to give other than the high
lights in the history of the Rassul tomb Pha-
roahs. Much more could be said about Thutmosis III. We must, however, refer to the fact
that he and his Queen erected the principal
Obelisks of Egypt, *including the Obelisk in Central Park, New York,* to which we have already
referred. A chiseled inscription of what the

*Thutmosis III,
who built the
Obelisk in our
Park, was found
in Rassul tomb.*

builder of it said on one of the great temples referring to these Obelisks, says:

"I sat in the Palace;
I remembered Him who fashioned me;
My heart led me to make Him two Obelisks
  whose points mingled with Heaven."

It then proceeds in substance to state that the architect was called and instructed to proceed to the granite quarries at the first cataract in Assuan to secure two gigantic shafts for the Obelisks; that he levied the necessary forced labor and began work early in February of the fifteenth year of the reign. By early August he had freed the huge blocks from the quarry, was able to employ the high water of the Nile and to tow them away. It then states that the precious metal was measured out by the peck like sacks of grain, there being nearly twelve bushels of electrum, which gave them brilliant tips when the sun rises in the horizon of heaven. Volumes after volumes are engraven in hieroglyphics, as well as upon papyrus, stating in great detail the military operations of Thutmosis III. Rich as were the spoils of battle, they were insignificant compared with the wealth awaiting the Pharaoh in some of his captured cities. In one alone nine hundred and twenty-four chariots, including those of the Kings of Kadesh; two hundred and thirty-eight horses, with thousands of cattle and horses, magnificent household furniture of the captured King, with immense quantities of gold and silver. It is thus the great his-

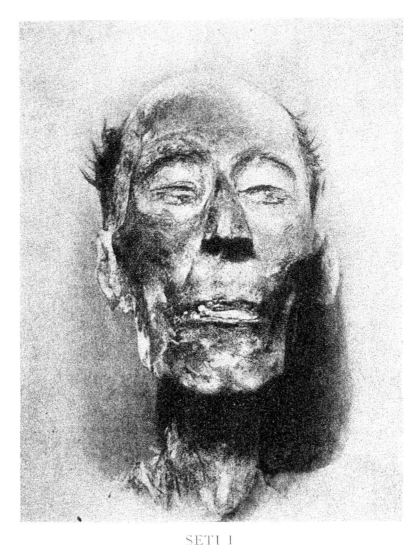

SETI I

FATHER of RAMESES, THE GREAT, as photographed
in the Cairo Museum, just as he looked entombed
more than 3300 years ago

tory goes on, telling of battles, victories, conquests, captives, spoils. It is interesting to note that Napoleon conducted a campaign through the same country from Egypt against Acre. The history of Thutmosis' campaign is given with as much detail almost as that of Napoleon, especially as to the principal facts of operations, but that which interests us the most is the fact that the Central Park *Obelisk* was made *by him*. On January 22, 1881, it was unveiled in the presence of twenty thousand spectators, nine thousand Free Masons paraded, and their Grand Master laid the foundation stone. It is the only Obelisk, excepting one, ever built by Thutmosis III containing its original pedestal and steps. The inscriptions chiseled deeply on the monolith dedicate it to Thutmosis III, historizing his titles with flattering epitaphs, and that it was erected before the Temple of Sun at Heliopolis by its great builder. This same Obelisk was erected over fifteen hundred years after its construction by Thutmosis in front of the Temple of Caesar in Alexandria.

9,000 free Masons paraded when Obelisk was first put up here.

For years it has been the pride of young America. Millions have stopped and wondered at its tremendous antiquity. It is a *contemporary of Moses,* who lived near it and saw it. Its hieroglyphic inscriptions in a dead language for more than two thousand years attest its absolute authenticity. It was used by the Caesars to adorn their Alexandrian temple even 1,500 years after it was built. Thutmosis III, its builder, has been resurrected from his tomb, where Rassul found him with six other Pharaohs, as we have shown. *He is as well preserved as is his Obelisk!*

Amosis and Amenophis found in Rassul tomb.

Amosis I reigned from 1580 to 1557 B. C., and Amenophis I from 1557 to 1545 B. C., with no particular distinction except the glory which attached to them as rulers of a great country wielding powerful sceptres and as masters of the world. Their bodies, too, with the other great Pharaohs mentioned, were in the care and possession of Rassul for over six years. He attached more importance to a handful of scarabs found scattered upon the floor of the tomb probably than he did to the seven Pharaohs themselves. He probably did not know their history. If he did, he did not know their value; even if he knew their value, he could not get them out alone. To summon assistance would disclose his secret. He simply followed the rule of life, which generally prevails, to get money in the easiest way possible, so he left the Pharaohs alone and helped himself to the scarabs, the *sacred* bug of the Egyptians, and sold them for money, with which he bought bread.

Seti I was the father of Rameses II, and died in 1621 B. C. In some respects he was the greatest of all the Pharaohs. As a warrior his activity was unrivalled. As a builder of monuments, which have ever since his day reflected glory upon the Empire over which he ruled, he was unexcelled. In cruelty he ranks in severity second to none in history, and as a patron of the religious temples, equalled by none. There is little

[60]

doubt that it was his cruelties with that of his son, Rameses the Great, and grandson, Menephtah, that are referred to as the Pharaohs of Oppression and Exodus in the Bible. If there is any uncertainty as to which part either one of the trio played in this, the world's greatest drama, there is no doubt some one or all of the three were the subjects of the Biblical reference concerning acts of slaughter, oppression and expulsion. His daughter rescued little Moses from the bullrushes, around which incident is interwoven a story of pathos and romance unequalled in profane or sacred history. He reigned jointly with his son, Rameses the Great, for more than fifty years. It must be remembered that his grandson, Menephtah, lived in Egypt about three years after the Exodus, according to Schmidt, an Egyptologist of great learning. Papyrus shows that he held control of the portion of Canaan, bordering on the sea, that in his eighth year there was carried into effect, according to Pharaoh's command, the passage of certain tribes of *Shasu,* from the land of Edom and from the Fortress Menephtah, which is situated in Succoth, to Pithon, in order to feed themselves and their herds on the possessions of the Pharaoh. Volumes of hieroglyphic history flash everywhere on engraven temples, tombs and monuments, showing his deeds of valor and of cruelty, which, in short, establish his rank among the most active and powerful monarchs the world ever saw. His body was taken with the six others described in this Chapter, from

Seti I, father of Rameses, and daughter, who rescued Moses.

[61]

the Rassul tomb at Dier-el-Bahari, in almost a perfect state of preservation. A photographic reproduction with that of his distinguished son, Rameses the Great, are presented in this book, showing their appearance. They need no description, the lens is more accurate and graphic than any word picture can give.

Valley of the Kings, where the Pharaohs' cemetery is located and
Tombs are found

CHAPTER VII.

The Tomb of Tut-ankh-Amen Has Justly Excited Anew the Wonder of the World

THE many years of toil and vast sums of money expended in the effort of Lord Carnarvon through the assistance of Mr. Carter, has been rewarded by success. The tomb of Tut-ankh-Amen is in the Valley of the Kings, and known by the Arabs as Biban-el-Mulak. The priceless treasures and perfect condition of the great quantity of funerary and household articles, as well as personal effects of the dead Pharaoh, again has *focused* the attention of the world upon Thebes. Thirty centuries ago that city, with its alleged one hundred golden gates and a populace said to be four millions, at the zenith of its power, attracted the attention of the whole world. Since then it has degenerated into nothing but a rich agricultural plain of tremendous ruins for miles in most directions, and inhabited only by miserable Arabs. The throne, chariots, gold and silver treasures and stones, which they are now lifting

Treasures and chariots found attracted attention of world in ancient times as now.

out of this sepulchre and buried for over thirty centuries, are what, even in those days, attracted the world as today. Indeed, a multitude of the articles found are of such exquisitely beautiful workmanship as to show conclusively that Tut-ankh-Amen wielded a sceptre from a throne unsurpassed in richness and elegance, if equalled by any yet found in the history of the world. It may interest the reader to know something of Tut-ankh-Amen, that is, who he was, when he reigned and what he did. The name of Tut-ankh-Amen, as appears by the inscriptions in the hieroglyphic history of Egypt, was given to him in honor of the Theban God, Ammon, forced on him as shown herein later, by priests of Ammon. It seems quite clear that his place was near the close of the eighteenth dynasty, 1350 B. C.; that his immediate successor was *Eye,* whose tomb is in the Valley of the Kings, found sometime since, unfinished and empty. Prior to Tut-ankh-Amen, Anenophis IV had endeavored to replace the old religion by the worship of a single God, namely, the *Sun*. This was directly opposed to the worship of Ammon in the great temple at Thebes, which had thrown all other temples into the shade for more than three centuries. We find that there was great agitation in the religious and political history and life of the monarchy at the time Tut-ankh-Amen commenced his reign. When he ascended the throne and *sat in the very chair recovered recently,* he signed an edict, transferring the Royal residence back to Thebes from Ikhnaton. After the death of

Name of Tut-Ankh-Amen forced on him by priests of Ammon.

Amenophis IV the chiseled inscriptions all over the Empire show internal commotions of a serious nature, resulting in the abolishment of the new one-God religion. It must be remembered that Tut-ankh-Amen reigned before the Rameses and, within one hundred years of their sovereignty. The inscriptions upon the tombs and temples of which there are many, show great tributes of vases, silver, gold, lapis-lazuli, turquoises and all the precious stones of the country, with horses and chariots as presents given Tut-ankh-Amen. We also find Egyptologists reading the chiseled engravings in hieroglyphical language, telling us that the Pharaoh received great embassies of negroes, both black and copper-colored from Ethiopia, drawn in a bullock-car, besides oxen, horses, and other animals. The negroes are represented as bringing many objects which show unusual refinement and the influence of Egyptian civilization upon foreign countries. It also appears that they subsequently brought chairs and other articles of furniture as offerings to Egypt from their Ethiopian cities. Curious enough, school and college histories and other standard works of literature, have long especially spoken of the fact that at the close of the eighteenth dynasty in which he, Tut-ankh-Amen, reigned, other countries gathered precious stones, gold and silver and offerings of all kinds and came to the throne of the Pharaoh and gave them as a token of their friendship and esteem. How little it may be said, when those studies were pursued by scholars young

Great tributes to Pharaohs found in their tombs.

*Treasures now
found often re-
ferred to by
poets and writers
as tributes to the
Pharaoh.*

and old and made the subject of educational and political reference, even up to within the last year, was it thought, that the tomb of one of the very last Pharaohs of the eighteenth Dynasty would be opened, and out of it taken several carloads or more of the priceless articles and offerings given as tributes to the reigning monarch, about which the students had read. Such a thing has happened, and today there is an absolute verification of the fact as romantically handed down to us since the discovery of the *Rosetta-stone.* One of the most important events in the whole political and religious history of the great kingdom, of which scholars have any account, was the spiritual change made by Amenophis IV in the life of the nation, when he abolished the worship of the Gods to whom the mighty temples of Egypt had been dedicated for many centuries. This so aroused the antagonism of the high priests of Ammon and other great temples at Thebes and throughout the nation generally, that internal war was waged. The prosperity of the nation was imperiled and its political contentions became imminent. Immediately upon the elevation of Tut-ankh-Amen, the throne was transferred back from *Akhetaton* to Thebes. His immediate predecessor was Sakere, who succeeded the great Ikhnaton, the most powerful of the Pharaohs opposed to the Temple devotees worshipping more than one God. The name of Tut-ankh-Amen means "the living image of Ammon." He was the son-in-law of Ikhnaton and had married the King's third daughter. Now the priestly party of the great temple was getting back fast to its old prestige of political power. Tut-ankh-Amen still continued to reside at Akhetaton, a small city not far from Thebes. It was not long, however, after his accession to the throne that he found it necessary to divest himself of adherence to the theory of a one-God religion. Although he had married Ikhnaton's daughter and resided in Akhetaton city, he felt obliged to and did, as a matter of fact, transfer back the court of his Empire to Thebes. It must be remembered that, for twenty years or more, Thebes had been abandoned as a Royal residence by the Pharaohs for the first in its long history of many centuries. It is strange, but incontestably true, as evidenced by a very great amount of hieroglyphic inscriptions, that the new city of Akhetaton, the recent seat of State, was obliged to maintain, after Tut-ankh-Amen ascended the throne and moved from there, a precarious existence. It made colored glass and faience, the manufacture of which was introduced by the King Ikhnaton. It was not long before the whole place went into ruins, and it is said that not a solitary soul was found upon its streets after Tut-ankh-Amen had gone to Thebes. The monumental inscriptions, and there are plenty of them, state that "even the roofs of the houses fell in and the walls tottered and collapsed, so that it became transformed into an abandoned city." The present place of *Tell-el-Amarna,* stands on the site of the old

Thebes, once abandoned as royal lresidence, but restored by Tut-Ankh-Amen.

[67]

Aton (short name for Akhetaton). Some diggers for antiques and possibly tombs, in 1885, found in an old brick room in this abandoned city where Tut-ankh-Amen lived, before he went to Thebes, three hundred letters and despatches, from which Egyptologists have been able to trace his correspondence and transactions with the potentates of Asia at that time, and a description of the gradual, but threatened dissolution of his kingdom. These letters and correspondence written on papyrus have all been well preserved. Now, there were other cities besides Aton, and they all utterly perished after the fall of him, who established Akhetaton and them as well. There was one which escaped, and that was Gem-Aton, in Nubia, far away. When Tut-ankh-Amen went back to Thebes, he was still spiritually inclined to the theory of one-God religion, and was more or less opposed to the priests of Ammon, but, their influence was so great and powerful that he finally yielded. The high priests again recommenced their worship in the great Temple, and other Temples about Thebes. His immediate predecessors had abandoned and destroyed the old festal calendar of *Karnak* and *Luxor*. He was humiliatingly obliged, however, to *restore* these festivals and to respect the temples. He was again obliged to restore the disfigured name of Ammon which had been taken off the temples by Ikhnaton. Then at last, came the one great Command made upon him by the high priests of Ammon, to which he in a dispirited way yielded. He was obliged to change his name to Tut-ankh-Amen, which thereafter he always carried and did so to his tomb, as we are daily learning. Tut-ankh-Amen means in hieroglphic language, as we have shown, "the living image of Ammon." If he possessed what are supposed to be the physical and spiritual characteristics of the God, of which he claimed he was an image, he must have been very attractive indeed.

Changed his name by command of priests.

As we have said before, he became a ruler of a great country when in the initial stage of dissolution, caused by internal strife over religious contentions. Egypt at that time extended from the Delta, that is, from the Mediterrean to the Fourth Cataract, towards Nubia. It is said that the Revolution in Egypt did not seriously affect Nubia's contribution of its annual dues to the Treasury at Thebes. Neither did it stop the flow of wealth from the North and from the East. The inscriptions at several places, as Egyptologists tell us, show that Ikhnaton's immediate successors fought a battle in Asia. The one who fought it was no other than Tut-ankh-Amen himself. He did not reign long. The reader must not become incredulous as to the certainty of historical details with which the history of the Pharaoh is written. It is blazoned forth on myriads of temples, tombs, mortuary chapels, and papyrus. Although the language in which it was written has been dead for more than twenty centuries, its meaning is now known and is as accurate as though written in Latin or English, and within the last year.

Already great praise is due Lord Carnarvon
and his able assistant, Mr. Carter, for the marvelous work and skill they have devoted to the
discovery of Tut-ankh-Amen's Tomb, and the
preservation of its contents. Lord Carnarvon has
shown the spirit of a gentleman of the highest
culture and ambition in spending a great sum of
money and time to illuminate the ancient history
of Egypt by searching for, and at last, opening
the royal Mausoleum of a Pharaoh. This has
taken, we understand, seven years of continuous
work, with a large number of diggers, skilfully
and patiently directed, in addition to all this, over
twenty years of preliminary surveys and study
to approximately locate the site for successful
operations, and he has at last been rewarded
with success. The entrance into the Tomb has
been a most solemn and sacred act. The task
before him has been attended with grave re-
sponsibility. He and his assistant have been,
and are fully conscious of the high dignity and
deep solemnity of the part they are playing in
this great *drama* staged in *Thebes,* with the
whole world as an enthusiastic audience. Our
reference to the wonderful sepulcher discovered
by Rassul in 1875 and disclosed in 1881, has
been given with no intent to belittle, by comparison, the vast importance or interest which attaches to the Tomb of Tut-ankh-Amen. Such
discovery by him necessarily forms the *first*
scene in the great Theban *drama* of resurrection, which is now being played at Thebes;
the *second* was that enacted by *Loret,* in 1898,

[70]

in opening the Tomb of Amenophis II; and now the curtain is up again in the *third* act, before a world-wide audience, with Lord Carnarvon unlocking the *Mausoleum* of *Tut-ankh-Amen,* the last great Pharaoh of the eighteenth Dynasty, sealed up tightly in a mountain rock over thirty-two centuries ago. One act finds its complement in the other. The three together form a drama of resurrection from the grave, unparalleled in all history, except the sacred one at Jerusalem, known of all men.

CPSIA information can be obtained at www.ICGtesting.com
Printed in the USA
BVOW061421070513

320115BV00004B/46/P

9 781162 585345